MacBook Seniors Guide

*Learn, Explore, and Master Your
Mac with Step-by-Step Instructions
and Troubleshooting Tips*

Gracie peter

1

TABLE OF CONTENT

Introduction

Welcome to a guide designed to simplify your journey with the MacBook, turning what may initially feel complex into something accessible and enjoyable. If you're new to the MacBook, whether it's your first time with an Apple device or you're transitioning from another platform, this book is created to make things easy. We'll break down each aspect of using a MacBook into steps that are straightforward and doable, ensuring that no prior experience is needed.

The purpose of this guide is to provide you with all the tools and knowledge necessary to feel comfortable with your MacBook. Too often, technology can feel intimidating, especially if you're not familiar with its unique features and functions. This guide aims to bridge that gap by presenting the essentials of your MacBook in a way that's easy to understand and even easier to apply. From turning on your device to mastering everyday tasks like browsing the internet, managing files, making video calls, and customizing settings, this book has been crafted to support you every step of the way.

This guide is specifically designed with seniors, beginners, and anyone new to MacBooks in mind. It assumes no prior technical knowledge, so you won't find any complex jargon or confusing instructions here. The explanations are simple and practical, using familiar language to make each step clear. For seniors, it's tailored to the pace and clarity that make learning comfortable, recognizing that not everyone has grown up surrounded by technology. If you're a beginner, it offers a gentle introduction to your MacBook's features, giving you time to build your confidence without feeling overwhelmed. And for those just getting started with their MacBook—regardless of age—it provides an overview of what you'll need to know to make the most of your device.

One of the unique aspects of this guide is its practical, hands-on approach. You're encouraged to use this book as you work through each part of your MacBook, tackling one small step at a time. Think of it as a companion that walks alongside you, offering clear instructions that you can follow as you go. If you prefer to read through a section first and try it later, that's perfectly fine too. The content is organized to let you move at your own pace, so you can revisit any part whenever you need a refresher. You don't need to go through every chapter in order if you're only interested in specific topics—each section stands on its own and offers practical help for specific tasks.

So, what can you expect as you go through this book? We'll start with the absolute basics, covering everything from setting up your MacBook to understanding its key features. By the time you've completed the initial chapters, you'll know how to navigate your desktop, find and open applications, and perform everyday tasks that form the foundation of using a MacBook. You'll also learn about core elements such as the trackpad, keyboard, and basic settings that will make the device feel like a natural extension of your daily routine.

Beyond the basics, this guide introduces the more advanced features of the MacBook that many users find helpful, especially for staying connected and organized. You'll discover how to use email, make video calls with family and friends, browse the internet safely, and manage your digital files. Each feature is broken down into manageable steps, with practical tips on how to make the most of these tools. This approach makes sure you're not just learning functions, but also understanding how they fit into your everyday life and can make your experience with the MacBook more rewarding.

Another focus of this book is security and privacy. As we go through the guide, you'll find helpful advice on keeping your MacBook safe from online threats, securing your personal information, and setting up protective measures like two-factor authentication. For beginners, these steps may feel new, but each explanation is crafted to make safety on your device feel straightforward and achievable. Learning to navigate your MacBook confidently means also knowing how to protect your data, so you can explore without worry.

Learning these basics offers more than just technical know-how—it can transform your experience with the MacBook into something enjoyable and empowering. Understanding how to use your MacBook doesn't just help you accomplish daily tasks; it can also open up new possibilities, from connecting with loved ones to exploring online interests. Whether you're staying in touch with family through FaceTime, organizing photos to preserve memories, or learning to browse the web for information, these skills will make using your MacBook feel rewarding and help you stay connected to what matters most to you.

Moreover, having confidence with your MacBook gives you a sense of independence. Once you've learned to manage basic functions on your own, you'll likely feel more in control and less dependent on others for help with technology. This guide aims to instill that confidence, enabling you to take on new tasks independently, one step at a time. As you move through each chapter, you'll be building your skills in a way that feels manageable and encouraging, reinforcing that you have everything you need to use your MacBook with ease.

Finally, while this book is filled with guidance on what your MacBook can do, remember that it's also a flexible tool. Technology should work for you, not the other way around, so feel free to pick and choose which features suit your needs. The MacBook is built to be versatile, so if certain tasks are more relevant to you than others, there's no need to explore every single feature. This guide is here to introduce you to the possibilities, but ultimately, you decide what feels most useful and meaningful.

This introduction is just the beginning of a supportive journey into learning and mastering your MacBook. Each page aims to build your confidence, knowledge, and ease of use, so that your experience with this device feels smooth, satisfying, and enjoyable. With this guide, you have everything you need to take your first steps into the world of MacBook, knowing that you're fully equipped to make it a positive and empowering experience.

Chapter 1: Getting Started with Your MacBook

Starting with your MacBook can feel both exciting and a bit overwhelming. Apple has designed the MacBook to be user-friendly, and this chapter will guide you through the basics, ensuring you feel comfortable and prepared. From unboxing to setting up essential security, each step will get you familiar with your new device and ready to explore its features confidently.

1.1 Unboxing and Setting Up

When you first unbox your MacBook, you'll find several key components included. Inside the box, there is the MacBook itself, which is the main device. Alongside it, you'll find a power adapter and charging cable, which are essential for keeping your MacBook charged. Depending on the model, you may also see a user guide or some basic instructions, which can be useful for quick reference. Taking a moment to check that all components are included will help ensure you have everything you need to get started.

Once you have all components ready, it's time to charge your MacBook. Begin by connecting the charging cable to the power adapter, then plug the adapter into a power source. On your MacBook, locate the charging port, which is usually on the side of the device. Plug in the charging cable, and you'll see a small light indicator on the cable or on the screen, letting you know that the device is charging.

It's a good idea to fully charge your MacBook before using it for the first time to ensure you can complete the setup process without interruptions.

Now that your MacBook is fully charged, it's time to power it on.

Locate the power button, which is often found in the upper-right corner of the keyboard, or if you have a newer model, simply opening the lid may turn it on automatically. Once powered on, the screen will light up, and you'll see the Apple logo, indicating that the MacBook is starting up. The initial setup screen will appear shortly, guiding you through the first steps to personalize your device. The MacBook's setup process is designed to be straightforward, so follow along on the screen, and you'll have it ready for use in no time.

1.2 Navigating the Setup Screen

As the setup screen loads, you'll be prompted to make some initial selections to customize your MacBook's settings. First, you'll be asked to select your preferred language. Scroll through the list, find the language you're comfortable with, and select it.

After choosing your language, you'll be asked to confirm your region or country. This setting ensures that your MacBook is configured correctly for local time, date formats, and language options, making it more convenient for everyday use.

The next step is connecting to Wi-Fi, which allows your MacBook to access the internet and download any updates needed during setup. Look for your Wi-Fi network on the list of available options, select it, and enter the password if prompted. Once connected, your MacBook will establish an internet connection, allowing you to proceed with the rest of the setup. If you encounter any trouble connecting, ensure your Wi-Fi network is active and that you have the correct password.

Signing in with or creating an Apple ID is an important step that follows. Your Apple ID is your key to accessing Apple services like iCloud, the App Store, and iMessage.

If you already have an Apple ID from an iPhone or iPad, you can sign in using those credentials. If not, you'll have the option to create a new one directly from the setup screen. Enter your details carefully, as this account will help you synchronize data, make app purchases, and recover your account if needed.

1.3 Essential Security Setup

Securing your MacBook from the start is important to protect your personal information. During setup, you'll be prompted to create a secure password. Choose a password that is easy for you to remember but difficult for others to guess. A secure password generally includes a mix of letters, numbers, and symbols. This password will be required whenever you wake up or log into your MacBook, adding a layer of protection to your device.

Once your password is set, enabling the "Find My Mac" feature is recommended.

This feature is part of Apple's iCloud services and allows you to locate your MacBook if it's ever lost or misplaced. If enabled, you can log into iCloud.com from another device and see your MacBook's location on a map, helping you retrieve it more easily. This feature also allows you to remotely lock or erase your device if it's lost, protecting your data from unauthorized access.

If your MacBook model supports it, you'll also have the option to set up Touch ID. Touch ID is a fingerprint recognition feature that allows you to unlock your MacBook quickly and securely by placing your finger on the sensor, which is usually integrated into the power button. Setting up Touch ID during the initial setup process is straightforward; follow the prompts on the screen, and your fingerprint will be saved as an additional way to access your MacBook securely.

1.4 MacBook Essentials Checklist

With the basics covered, it's useful to review a quick checklist of tasks to complete for an optimized setup. These steps ensure that your MacBook is personalized to suit your preferences and ready for regular use. Confirm that you're connected to Wi-Fi, signed into or created an Apple ID, and that you've set a secure password. If available, enable Find My Mac and set up Touch ID to enhance security.

Once your MacBook is secured, you can adjust some basic settings to customize the user experience. Start with the display settings, where you can modify brightness and resolution. Adjust the sound settings to set volume levels that suit you, which can be helpful for notifications and media playback. Customizing these initial settings will make your MacBook feel more comfortable and tailored to your preferences.

Completing these setup steps puts you in a great position to begin exploring your MacBook's features. With a secure, personalized setup, you're ready to make the most of what your MacBook has to offer.

Chapter 2: Exploring the MacBook Interface

The MacBook's interface is designed to be intuitive and user-friendly, making it easy to navigate once you get the hang of its main features. This chapter will guide you through the essential elements of the desktop, trackpad, and keyboard, and provide you with tips for managing applications and customizing your workspace. Becoming familiar with these tools will allow you to work efficiently and comfortably, giving you a strong foundation for exploring all that your MacBook can offer.

2.1 Desktop Overview

The desktop is the first thing you see when you log into your MacBook, serving as the central workspace for all your activities.

Three main elements on the desktop will help you navigate and access files and applications: the Finder, Dock, and Menu Bar.

The Finder is the MacBook's file management system, which allows you to access, organize, and search for files. You can open Finder by clicking on its icon, a happy face symbol located on the left side of the Dock. Finder windows display your files and folders, giving you easy access to documents, downloads, and other storage areas. Within Finder, you can create folders to organize files, move items around, and search for specific documents using the search bar at the top.

The Dock, located at the bottom of the screen, is a collection of icons that give you quick access to frequently used applications. It's fully customizable, allowing you to add or remove apps based on your preferences. The Dock also displays any open applications, so you can switch between them easily by clicking on the corresponding icon.

On the right side of the Dock, you'll find the Trash icon, which is where deleted files are stored until you choose to empty it.

The Menu Bar sits at the top of the screen and provides a variety of options based on the active application. On the left side, you'll see the Apple menu, which contains important system functions such as shutting down or restarting your MacBook. To the right of the Apple menu, the menu items change according to the app you're using, allowing you to access features specific to that app. On the right side of the Menu Bar, you'll find quick settings like Wi-Fi, battery status, sound, and date and time.

Together, these elements—Finder, Dock, and Menu Bar—form the backbone of the MacBook interface, helping you stay organized and access tools with ease.

2.2 Using the Trackpad and Keyboard

The MacBook's trackpad and keyboard are designed to work seamlessly with macOS, making navigation smooth and efficient. The trackpad, in particular, is a powerful tool that supports a variety of gestures for quick actions.

Common trackpad gestures can simplify many tasks. For example, a single tap acts as a click, while a two-finger swipe scrolls through pages or lists. If you spread two fingers apart on the trackpad, you can zoom in, similar to how you would on a smartphone. A three-finger swipe up opens Mission Control, which displays all open windows and apps, allowing you to switch between them easily. Experimenting with these gestures will help you navigate faster and make the most of your MacBook's capabilities.

The keyboard also has shortcuts that can be quite helpful. For instance, pressing "Command" and "C" at the same time copies selected text or items, while "Command" and

"V" pastes them. If you press "Command" and "Q," it will quit the current application, while "Command" and "Tab" allows you to switch between open applications. The function keys, located along the top row of the keyboard, offer quick access to volume controls, brightness adjustments, and other settings, depending on your MacBook model. Knowing these shortcuts and function keys can save you time and make your work on the MacBook more efficient.

2.3 Accessing and Managing Applications

MacBook applications are accessible in several ways, allowing you to choose the method that feels most natural. You can open applications directly from the Dock by clicking on the app icon, which will immediately launch it. For apps that aren't on the Dock, you can open Finder, go to the "Applications" folder, and double-click on the app you want to use.

To keep your desktop uncluttered, it's helpful to understand how to minimize and close applications.

Minimizing an app will keep it open but hide it from view, storing it in the Dock. You can minimize an application by clicking the yellow button in the top-left corner of the window. Closing an app, on the other hand, can be done by clicking the red button in the same location, which will close the window but may keep the app running in the background. To fully quit an application, press "Command" and "Q" or right-click on the app icon in the Dock and select "Quit."

Spotlight Search is another powerful tool for finding applications, files, and other information on your MacBook. You can activate Spotlight by clicking the magnifying glass icon in the upper-right corner of the Menu Bar or by pressing "Command" and "Space" simultaneously.

Type the name of the app, file, or even a specific phrase, and Spotlight will display relevant results instantly. This feature is particularly useful if you have many applications or files, as it allows you to locate them quickly without navigating through folders.

2.4 Customizing Your Desktop

Customizing your desktop can make the MacBook feel more personal and tailored to your style. You can start by changing the wallpaper, which serves as the background for your desktop. To do this, right-click on the desktop and select "Change Desktop Background." You'll have options to choose from Apple's default images or your own photos, allowing you to add a personal touch to your workspace.

The Dock is also customizable, and you can add or remove applications to suit your needs.

To add an app, open the Applications folder in Finder, then drag the desired app icon to the Dock. To remove an app, simply click and drag its icon out of the Dock, then release. Customizing the Dock this way ensures that your frequently used applications are always within easy reach, while keeping your desktop neat and organized.

You can also adjust your MacBook's screen saver settings, which adds a layer of visual interest when your device is idle. To set up or change the screen saver, go to "System Preferences," then select "Desktop & Screen Saver." From there, you can browse various screen saver styles and choose the one that appeals to you. Setting up a screen saver is not only decorative but can also help preserve the screen when your MacBook is not in use.

By adjusting these desktop settings, you create a comfortable and personalized work environment that enhances your MacBook experience.

The ability to customize your space, combined with knowledge of the core elements like Finder, Dock, and Menu Bar, gives you the flexibility to navigate your MacBook confidently and efficiently.

Chapter 3: Connecting to the Internet and Staying Secure

Getting connected to the internet is one of the first steps to fully using your MacBook, as it opens up a world of information, entertainment, and communication. However, with connectivity comes the need for security, especially in today's digital world. This chapter covers how to set up Wi-Fi and Bluetooth, browse the web safely, protect your MacBook from online threats, and, if necessary, set up parental controls for safe family use. These steps will help you maintain a secure, reliable connection, allowing you to use your MacBook confidently.

3.1 Setting Up Wi-Fi and Bluetooth

Connecting to Wi-Fi is essential for accessing the internet, and setting it up is simple.

Start by clicking on the Wi-Fi icon located in the upper-right corner of the Menu Bar.

When you click this icon, a list of available Wi-Fi networks will appear. Select your network from the list, then enter the Wi-Fi password if prompted. Once you enter the correct password, your MacBook will connect to the network, and you'll see the Wi-Fi icon change to show the connection is active. Your MacBook will remember this network, so you won't need to re-enter the password next time you connect. In cases where you are using a secure or public network, ensure that the connection is private and requires a password for added security.

Bluetooth is another valuable feature on your MacBook, allowing you to connect wireless devices like a keyboard, mouse, or headphones. To turn on Bluetooth, open "System Preferences" from the Apple menu, then select "Bluetooth." You'll see a list of nearby Bluetooth devices.

To connect, make sure your device is turned on and set to "pairing mode" (usually indicated by a blinking light). When it appears on the MacBook's list of available devices, click "Connect." After pairing, your MacBook will remember the device, and it will connect automatically in the future when both the device and Bluetooth are turned on.

3.2 Browsing the Web Safely

Safari is the default web browser on your MacBook and is designed for a secure, smooth browsing experience. To open Safari, click its icon in the Dock. Once open, you can enter a website's address or search term in the address bar at the top. Safari also provides convenient features like bookmarks, which let you save favorite sites for quick access, and tabs, allowing you to open multiple websites simultaneously in a single window.

As you browse, familiarize yourself with the browser's layout to make navigation easier.

To ensure a secure browsing experience, it's important to adjust a few settings in Safari.

Begin by opening Safari, then go to the Safari menu in the upper-left corner and select "Preferences." Here, you'll find the "Privacy" and "Security" tabs. Under "Privacy," you can enable settings to prevent websites from tracking your browsing behavior, which adds an extra layer of privacy. In the "Security" tab, make sure options like "Warn when visiting a fraudulent website" are enabled. This setting will alert you if Safari detects a potentially unsafe site, helping protect you from scams and phishing attempts.

Setting up secure browsing is a simple yet effective way to keep your online experience safe. Avoid clicking on suspicious links or pop-ups, especially those that seem to request personal information or direct you to unfamiliar websites.

Safe browsing habits, combined with Safari's built-in security features, will help you enjoy the internet without exposing your MacBook to unnecessary risks.

3.3 Must-Know Security Tips

With internet use comes the possibility of encountering scams, phishing, and other online threats. Staying informed and vigilant can help you avoid these issues. One important rule is to never provide personal information (like your password or credit card details) to unfamiliar sites or sources. If you receive emails that request personal information or have suspicious links, it's best to delete them or mark them as spam. Many phishing emails are designed to look legitimate, but they often contain telltale signs like spelling errors or urgent demands for information.

Enabling two-factor authentication (2FA) on your Apple ID is another effective way to enhance security.

Two-factor authentication adds a second layer of protection to your account, requiring both your password and a verification code sent to your phone or another trusted device. To set up 2FA, go to "System Preferences," then click on "Apple ID" and select "Password & Security." Here, you'll see an option to turn on two-factor authentication. Once enabled, you'll receive a code each time you log in on a new device, making it more difficult for unauthorized users to access your account.

Your MacBook also includes a built-in firewall, which adds a layer of protection against unauthorized access. To check that your firewall is active, open "System Preferences" and select "Security & Privacy." Under the "Firewall" tab, click "Turn On Firewall" if it's not already enabled. The firewall helps block potential intrusions from malicious websites and applications, keeping your MacBook more secure.

These combined security measures will give you peace of mind and help protect your personal information.

3.4 Setting Up Parental Controls

If you're sharing your MacBook with family members, particularly children, setting up parental controls can help ensure a safe digital environment. To activate these controls, go to "System Preferences" and select "Screen Time." Screen Time allows you to set limits on app usage, restrict access to specific websites, and control various settings for different users on your MacBook.

Once in Screen Time, click "Options" in the lower-left corner, then "Turn On" Screen Time. From there, you can choose to set up restrictions for specific users or create a passcode to prevent changes. Under "Content & Privacy Restrictions," you'll find options to restrict explicit content, limit web browsing to specific sites, and control app downloads.

For instance, you might allow access only to educational or child-friendly websites, blocking any potentially inappropriate content. To customize these restrictions, simply toggle the settings to your preference.

If you'd like to restrict the use of certain apps, you can set daily time limits for specific categories, like social media or games. Screen Time will notify the user when the set time limit is reached, helping to manage usage. These parental controls are a useful feature for family MacBooks, giving you control over what content is accessible while providing peace of mind. Whether used for children or other family members, Screen Time allows you to create a secure and appropriate environment on your MacBook.

Following these steps will ensure that you have a safe and secure experience on your MacBook. Connecting to the internet, browsing responsibly, setting up strong security measures, and using parental controls where needed all contribute to a secure and enjoyable digital environment.

Chapter 4: Staying Connected with Communication Tools

Your MacBook comes equipped with various tools to help you stay connected with friends, family, and colleagues. Whether it's through email, instant messaging, video calls, or even social media, your MacBook has built-in features that make communication seamless and straightforward. This chapter will guide you through setting up and using these essential communication tools, helping you stay in touch without hassle.

4.1 Setting Up Email Accounts

The Mail app on your MacBook allows you to manage all your email accounts in one convenient place. To add an email account, open the Mail app from the Dock or Finder.

When the app opens for the first time, you'll be prompted to add an email account. Choose your email provider from the list, such as iCloud, Gmail, or Yahoo, then click "Continue." If your provider isn't listed, select "Other Mail Account" and enter your account details manually.

Once you select your provider, enter your email address and password. The Mail app will then automatically configure the settings for most popular email services. If you're using a less common provider, you may need to enter additional information like the incoming and outgoing server details, which you can typically find on your email provider's website. After entering the necessary information, click "Sign In" to complete the setup.

The Mail app will synchronize with your email account, displaying your messages and allowing you to send and receive emails directly from your MacBook.

If you have multiple email accounts, you can add them all to the Mail app for easy access.

To add another account, go to the Mail menu at the top of the screen, select "Add Account," and repeat the setup process for each account. Once you have multiple accounts set up, you can switch between them by clicking on the desired inbox in the sidebar. This way, all your emails are organized in one place, making it easy to manage both personal and work-related messages.

4.2 Sending Messages with iMessage

iMessage is Apple's instant messaging service, allowing you to send texts, photos, and files to other Apple users. To set up iMessage, open the Messages app from the Dock or Applications folder. If it's your first time using Messages on your MacBook, you'll be prompted to sign in with your Apple ID. Enter your Apple ID and password, then follow the on-screen instructions to activate iMessage.

Once iMessage is set up, you can start a conversation by clicking the "New Message" icon, which looks like a pencil and paper, in the upper-left corner of the Messages window. Type the name, email address, or phone number of the person you want to message, as long as they are also using an Apple device. You can type your message in the text box at the bottom of the window and press "Return" on your keyboard to send it.

In addition to text messages, iMessage allows you to send photos, videos, and files with ease. To share a photo or file, click the small camera icon next to the text box and select the file you want to send. This makes it easy to share moments or important documents instantly. You can also create group chats by adding multiple recipients to a message, which is perfect for family updates or coordinating with friends.

4.3 Making Video Calls with FaceTime

FaceTime is Apple's video and audio calling service, and it's built into every MacBook. With FaceTime, you can make high-quality video and audio calls to other Apple users, such as friends or family members who have an iPhone, iPad, or another MacBook. To set up FaceTime, open the FaceTime app from the Dock or Finder, then sign in with your Apple ID if prompted.

Once you're signed in, you'll see a simple interface with a search bar where you can enter the name, phone number, or email address of the person you want to call. As long as they're registered with FaceTime, you can initiate either a video or audio call. To start a video call, click the video camera icon next to their contact name, or select the phone icon to make an audio call if you prefer voice only.

You can also manage your FaceTime contacts by adding frequently called people to your

"Favorites" list, making it easier to find them quickly. To add someone to Favorites, simply click the "Add to Favorites" option next to their name in your contact list. FaceTime also has a recent calls section, so you can redial your most recent contacts with just a click. If you need to switch from an audio to a video call during a conversation, FaceTime makes it easy to do so with a quick click.

4.4 Managing Social Media (Optional)

If you enjoy using social media, your MacBook makes it easy to access these platforms through Safari or any other browser of your choice. Although there isn't a dedicated social media app on the MacBook, you can visit websites like Facebook, Twitter, Instagram, and LinkedIn directly through your web browser. To access a social media site, open Safari from the Dock, type the name of the site into the address bar, and press "Return."

For a smooth social media experience, consider bookmarking your favorite sites in Safari.

This will allow you to access them quickly without typing the address every time. To bookmark a site, click the "Share" button in Safari's toolbar, then select "Add Bookmark." You can organize bookmarks into folders or add them to your Favorites, so they're easily accessible from Safari's home screen.

While social media can be a great way to stay connected, it's important to keep safety in mind. Avoid sharing personal information, like your home address or phone number, on public profiles, and be cautious about accepting friend requests from unfamiliar people. Adjusting your privacy settings on each platform is also recommended to limit who can see your posts and profile information. By staying mindful of these tips, you can enjoy a secure social media experience on your MacBook.

Your MacBook's communication tools are versatile and designed to help you stay connected with ease. With email, iMessage, FaceTime, and even social media access, you have everything you need to communicate effectively, whether it's for personal use or connecting with colleagues. Embracing these tools not only enhances your digital experience but also keeps you connected with the people who matter most.

Chapter 5: Mastering Everyday Tasks

5.1 Browsing the Internet with Safari

Using Safari on your MacBook provides a straightforward way to access the internet, making it easy to find information, connect with others, or enjoy online entertainment. When you open Safari, you'll notice the address bar at the top of the screen, where you can type either a website's address or keywords for a search. This feature allows you to reach specific websites or use a search engine like Google to explore topics. Safari's auto-suggestions appear as you type, offering related options to help you locate what you're looking for without needing to type everything out completely.

Safari supports tabs, allowing you to open multiple sites at once and switch between them easily. Tabs appear as separate "cards" at the top, which you can click to move from one page to another. If you're researching a topic and want to reference several sites, tabs let you keep them all open without needing to close and reopen them. This approach keeps your workspace organized and efficient, and you can close any tabs you no longer need by clicking the small "X" on each tab.

One of Safari's most useful features is bookmarking, which helps you save frequently visited websites for quick access. To bookmark a page, simply click the "Share" icon (a square with an arrow pointing up) and select "Add Bookmark." You'll then be prompted to choose a folder for organizing bookmarks. For instance, you could have folders for news sites, shopping sites, or personal blogs, keeping everything neatly organized.

Bookmarked sites can be accessed through the "Bookmarks" menu, saving time when revisiting favorites.

Safari also allows you to adjust settings to protect your privacy. In Safari's "Preferences," found in the "Safari" menu, you can access security settings under the "Privacy" tab.

Options like "Prevent cross-site tracking" stop websites from tracking your browsing activity. Safari also offers a "Fraudulent Website Warning," which alerts you if you attempt to access a suspicious or potentially harmful site. These features make browsing safer and reduce the likelihood of accidentally sharing information with unknown parties.

If you enjoy reading without distractions, Safari includes a "Reader" mode, which removes ads and other extras from articles. Simply click the "Reader" button in the address bar, and Safari will present a clean, easy-to-read version of the page's content. Reader mode is particularly helpful when viewing articles, as it minimizes distractions and improves readability.

5.2 Organizing and Managing Files in Finder

The Finder application on a MacBook is essential for accessing and managing all the files on your device. When you open Finder, you'll see a left sidebar displaying categories like "Applications," "Downloads," "Documents," and "Desktop," which are quick access points to different types of files. This layout allows you to locate files by navigating through these folders, saving you the effort of searching manually across your system. You can open Finder by clicking the happy face icon located in the Dock.

Finder offers flexible organization tools to make your file management easier. For instance, creating folders is a simple way to organize files by project, type, or any other category you prefer. To create a folder, click "File" at the top of the screen, then "New Folder."

You can then name the folder and start moving files into it by dragging and dropping. Custom folders help maintain order, especially if you have many files and documents to keep track of.

In addition to standard folders, Finder includes the option to add color-coded tags to files and folders. Tags provide a visual aid for quickly locating files based on color. For example, you could assign a red tag to urgent documents or a blue tag for personal photos. Tags can be applied by right-clicking on a file, choosing "Tags," and selecting a color. You can even create custom tags to suit specific needs, allowing for a high level of personalization.

Finder also makes it easy to search for specific files using the search bar in the upper right corner. This search function allows you to enter a filename or keyword, and Finder will show matching results instantly. If you need to narrow down results further, you can use filters such as "Kind" (to search for file types like

PDFs or images) or "Date" (to find recently modified files). These filters can be especially useful when dealing with large numbers of files, making the search process fast and accurate.

Another valuable feature within Finder is the "Quick Look" option, which lets you preview a file without fully opening it. By pressing the spacebar while a file is selected, you can view its contents immediately. This feature is handy for browsing through photos, documents, or PDFs quickly, helping you confirm the right file before opening it in a separate application. Once you're familiar with Finder's features, managing files on your MacBook becomes an intuitive, streamlined process.

5.3 Using Calendar for Scheduling

The Calendar app on your MacBook is a robust tool for managing appointments, events, and reminders, making it simple to organize your daily, weekly, and monthly schedule.

When you open Calendar, you can see different views: daily, weekly, monthly, or yearly, depending on how you prefer to plan. The monthly view is particularly helpful for seeing a big-picture view of upcoming commitments, while the daily view allows you to focus on specific tasks and events.

Adding an event in Calendar is straightforward. Simply click on the desired date and time, then enter details for the event, such as title, location, and duration. You can also invite others by adding their email addresses, which sends an invitation through their Apple devices or email accounts. Calendar lets you set reminders for events, either through notifications or email, ensuring you're reminded of important dates or deadlines in advance.

The Calendar app also allows for multiple calendars, which is helpful for organizing various areas of your life.

For example, you might have one calendar for personal events, another for work, and a third for family activities. Each calendar can be color-coded, so events are visually distinct, making it easier to differentiate between types of commitments. You can toggle these calendars on and off to focus on specific parts of your schedule.

One of Calendar's convenient features is its ability to sync across devices, ensuring that changes made on your MacBook appear on your iPhone, iPad, or other Apple devices. If you add an event on your MacBook, it will automatically appear on your iPhone if both devices are signed in with the same Apple ID. This seamless integration makes it easy to manage your schedule, whether you're at home or on the go.

For those who collaborate with others or work on shared projects, Calendar allows you to create shared calendars.

This feature is useful for family planning, team projects, or any situation where you need a group to stay updated on events. You can adjust permissions for shared calendars, allowing others to view or edit events as needed. Overall, Calendar is a versatile tool that keeps your schedule organized and accessible.

5.4 Taking Notes with the Notes App

The Notes app on your MacBook is a simple yet powerful tool for capturing ideas, lists, and reminders. When you open Notes, you'll see a list of previous notes in the sidebar, allowing you to quickly access and organize your thoughts. You can start a new note by clicking the "New Note" button, and from there, type out anything you want to remember. Notes are saved automatically, so you don't need to worry about losing information.

Notes also supports formatting options, which make organizing content easier.

You can add bulleted or numbered lists, bold text for emphasis, or even insert tables to organize data within your note. These options provide a flexible structure for keeping your notes clear and easy to follow. If you have a long list of tasks or ideas, adding bullet points can help break down information into manageable sections.

One useful feature of Notes is the ability to add attachments, such as photos, documents, or website links. You can drag files directly into a note or use the "Add Attachment" option to include additional information. This feature is particularly useful for collecting all relevant details in one place. For example, if you're planning a trip, you could include images, itineraries, and web links to create a comprehensive reference.

With Notes, organization is simple. You can create folders to categorize notes based on topics like "Work," "Personal," or "Shopping Lists."

These folders keep related notes grouped, so you can find what you need quickly. Additionally, Notes can be synced with iCloud, making your notes accessible across all Apple devices. If you start a note on your MacBook, you can continue working on it from your iPhone, ensuring you always have your notes with you.

For added security, Notes allows you to lock specific notes with a password. If you're storing sensitive information, like account numbers or private ideas, password protection prevents unauthorized access. To enable this, simply select the note you want to secure, then choose "Lock Note." You'll be prompted to set a password, providing extra security for important information.

Overall, the Notes app is a practical tool for capturing and organizing information, with flexible features that make it adaptable to a variety of tasks.

Chapter 6: Staying Organized with Productivity Tools

6.1 Managing Reminders and To-Do Lists

Staying on top of tasks and responsibilities becomes easier with the Reminders app on your MacBook. This tool is designed to help you organize your to-do lists and set reminders for important deadlines, tasks, and events. When you open Reminders, you'll find a clean, intuitive layout with a list of tasks on the right and categories on the left. You can start by creating a new reminder by clicking the "New Reminder" button or simply typing directly into the list.

Each reminder can be customized with specific details, such as due dates, priority levels, and additional notes, making it easy to track tasks accurately.

One of Reminders' strengths is its ability to group tasks into lists. You can create separate lists for different areas of your life, like "Work," "Home," or "Groceries," so tasks remain organized and easy to access. Each list can be color-coded, allowing you to visually differentiate them, which can be helpful if you have multiple projects or areas of focus. You can also create "smart lists," which automatically organize reminders based on criteria like due dates or flagged importance.

Setting up notifications for reminders ensures you don't miss important deadlines or tasks. For each reminder, you can choose to receive a notification at a specific time, date, or location. For example, if you have a reminder to pick up groceries, you can set it to alert you when you arrive at the store.

This location-based feature can be particularly useful for errands or tasks that require you to be in a specific place.

Reminders can also sync across your Apple devices using iCloud. This means any changes you make on your MacBook will appear on your iPhone, iPad, or Apple Watch, ensuring you have your tasks at hand wherever you go. If you share tasks with family members or colleagues, Reminders lets you create shared lists, allowing others to see tasks and even mark them as complete. This feature is helpful for collaborative projects or shared household tasks, making it easy for everyone involved to stay updated.

6.2 Using Contacts to Keep Track of People

The Contacts app on your MacBook serves as a central location for managing details about the people in your life.

You can store information like phone numbers, addresses, email addresses, birthdays, and even notes about each person. Opening Contacts brings up a simple interface where you can add new entries, organize contacts into groups, and easily search for specific individuals when needed.

To add a new contact, click the "+" button and enter the person's details, such as name, phone number, and email. You can also add custom fields for information like social media handles or work titles, creating a comprehensive contact card for each individual. Adding notes to contact cards allows you to remember important details or personal preferences, making it easier to maintain relationships.

Organizing contacts into groups is another feature that helps you stay organized. For instance, you can create groups like "Family," "Work," or "Friends" to keep contacts grouped by category.

This setup makes it easy to send group emails or messages without manually selecting each person. Groups also help you locate contacts quickly, especially if your list is extensive.

One of Contacts' useful features is integration with other apps. For example, birthdays added to contacts will automatically appear in your Calendar, ensuring you remember important dates. Contacts also syncs with iCloud, so your address book is updated across all Apple devices. If you add a new contact on your iPhone, it will instantly appear on your MacBook, allowing for seamless access to contacts anywhere.

6.3 Working with Photos and Albums

The Photos app on your MacBook provides a convenient way to organize and view all your photos and videos. When you open Photos, you'll see all your images arranged in a grid format, with options to sort them by date or event.

The app automatically groups photos into categories like "Memories" and "Favorites," making it easy to find specific moments and highlight cherished images.

Photos allows you to create albums to organize images by theme, event, or category. For example, you could create an album for a vacation, a family gathering, or a project. To create an album, simply click the "+" icon and select "Album," then drag and drop photos into the album to organize them. Albums help keep your photos in order, so you don't have to scroll through all your images every time you want to revisit a specific event or theme.

Editing tools within Photos give you the ability to enhance and adjust your images. You can adjust brightness, contrast, and color balance, crop or straighten images, and apply filters for different effects. For more advanced editing, Photos includes options like "Retouch" for removing minor blemishes and "Red-Eye" correction to improve the quality of your pictures. These tools allow you to personalize your photos, making them look their best without needing complex software.

The Photos app also syncs with iCloud, ensuring your photos are backed up and available across all Apple devices. This feature lets you view and manage your photo library from any device, whether you're using your MacBook, iPhone, or iPad. If you enable the "iCloud Photos" setting, any photos taken on your iPhone will automatically upload to the Photos app on your MacBook, making organization seamless. Additionally, iCloud offers shared albums, which allow you to share specific photos with friends and family. Shared albums enable others to contribute their photos to an album, creating a collaborative collection of memories.

6.4 Creating Documents in Pages

Pages, Apple's word-processing software, is designed for creating and editing documents on your MacBook. When you open Pages, you can start from a blank document or choose from a variety of templates for letters, reports, resumes, and more. Templates provide professionally designed layouts, so all you need to do is enter your content. This feature can be particularly helpful if you're new to creating documents, as it removes the need to format everything from scratch.

Creating a document in Pages is intuitive. The toolbar at the top offers a range of options to customize your text, such as font style, size, color, and alignment. Pages also includes tools for inserting elements like images, tables, and shapes, allowing you to add visual elements to your work. For example, if you're creating a report, you can insert graphs or charts to visually represent data. The app makes it easy to customize layouts and styles to suit your needs, providing a polished look to your documents.

Pages also supports collaboration, allowing you to share documents with others and edit together in real-time.

If you're working on a project with a colleague, you can send them a link to the document and enable editing permissions. This feature makes Pages ideal for team projects or any situation where multiple people need to contribute. Each contributor's changes are highlighted, making it easy to see who has modified what, ensuring clear communication and efficient teamwork.

When it's time to share your document, Pages offers a variety of export options. You can save your work as a PDF, Word document, or even an ePub file for reading on e-readers. This flexibility makes Pages compatible with other platforms, allowing you to send documents to people who may not use Apple products. With these features, Pages becomes a versatile tool for all your writing and document creation needs.

Chapter 7: Enhancing Accessibility Features

7.1 Adjusting Display and Text Sizes

Making the display and text more comfortable to read is one of the key accessibility features on a MacBook, allowing users to customize their screen for better visibility. To adjust the display and text size, start by opening "System Preferences" and selecting "Displays." Here, you'll find options to change the display resolution. For a larger, more readable display, you can select a scaled resolution that increases the size of items on the screen, making icons, text, and images appear larger.

For further adjustments, you can customize text sizes in specific apps and system areas. For example, if you want larger text in Finder, open Finder, click "View," then "Show View

Options," and increase the text size for files and folders.

Safari and other apps also offer customizable text size options, often found in the app's preferences. Additionally, the "Zoom" feature under "Accessibility" in System Preferences allows you to magnify parts of the screen as needed, which is particularly helpful for reading small text or viewing detailed images. By experimenting with these settings, you can find a comfortable display size that suits your needs and enhances readability.

7.2 Using VoiceOver for Screen Reading

VoiceOver is a built-in screen reader on your MacBook that reads out text, menus, and other screen elements, allowing you to navigate and interact with your computer using audio cues. To activate VoiceOver, go to "System Preferences," select "Accessibility," and choose "VoiceOver" from the menu.

You can turn it on by clicking "Enable VoiceOver" or by pressing "Command + F5." Once VoiceOver is enabled, it will begin describing elements on the screen, reading aloud the content as you move through apps and menus.

VoiceOver includes several customization options to make it work exactly the way you need. You can adjust the speaking rate, pitch, and volume to make it more comfortable to listen to, as well as choose different voices to match your preference. The VoiceOver Utility, accessible through System Preferences, provides an in-depth menu where you can fine-tune settings, including verbosity (how much detail is read aloud), navigation styles, and braille support if you're using a compatible braille display.

Navigating with VoiceOver relies on keyboard commands, known as VoiceOver commands, which make it easy to move around your MacBook without using a mouse or trackpad.

For instance, pressing "Control + Option + Right Arrow" moves you to the next item, while "Control + Option + Left Arrow" takes you to the previous one. Mastering these commands enables efficient use of VoiceOver, giving you full control over your MacBook through spoken feedback.

7.3 Setting Up Dictation and Speech Commands

For users who prefer hands-free typing or need assistance with text input, the MacBook offers a Dictation feature that converts spoken words into text. To set up Dictation, open "System Preferences," select "Keyboard," then choose the "Dictation" tab. Turn on Dictation, and select whether you'd like to enable Enhanced Dictation, which allows offline speech-to-text functionality. Once enabled, you can start using Dictation by pressing the "Fn" key twice (or another specified shortcut).

Begin speaking, and your words will appear on the screen in real time.

Dictation is ideal for typing longer documents, quick notes, or messages without manually typing. It also supports basic punctuation and formatting commands. For example, saying "comma" or "period" will add the respective punctuation mark, while commands like "new paragraph" and "new line" help organize text for readability. Dictation recognizes these commands intuitively, making it easy to transition from spoken instructions to neatly formatted text.

In addition to Dictation, macOS includes Voice Control, a more advanced feature that lets you control your MacBook with spoken commands. To enable Voice Control, go to "System Preferences," select "Accessibility," and choose "Voice Control." Once activated, Voice Control allows you to perform various tasks, such as opening apps, clicking on-screen items, and typing.

By saying commands like "Open Safari" or "Click OK," you can navigate the MacBook hands-free. Voice Control is particularly useful for those who may have limited mobility, offering a comprehensive alternative to traditional mouse and keyboard navigation.

7.4 Customizing Keyboard and Trackpad Settings

MacBook's keyboard and trackpad settings can be customized to suit your preferences and accessibility needs. For the keyboard, go to "System Preferences" and choose "Keyboard." Here, you can adjust settings such as key repeat rate and delay, which can be helpful if you prefer to type more slowly or want to avoid accidental repeated keystrokes. For those who benefit from an on-screen keyboard, macOS includes one under "Accessibility" that you can enable in System Preferences, providing a clickable alternative to the physical keyboard.

If typing is challenging, the "Sticky Keys" and "Slow Keys" options under Accessibility can make typing easier. Sticky Keys allow you to press keys sequentially rather than simultaneously for commands, which is helpful for users who find it difficult to press multiple keys at once. Slow Keys, on the other hand, add a delay between pressing a key and the computer registering the input, reducing accidental keystrokes.

Trackpad customization is found under "System Preferences" in the "Trackpad" section, where you can adjust tracking speed, tap-to-click sensitivity, and enable gestures. Enabling tap-to-click allows you to simply tap the trackpad instead of pressing down, which may be more comfortable for some users. The trackpad also supports gestures like swiping with two fingers to scroll, pinching to zoom, and rotating with your fingers to turn images.

These gestures can be turned on or off depending on your preferences.

By customizing the keyboard and trackpad settings, you can create a setup that aligns with your comfort and accessibility requirements, allowing for a smoother, more efficient experience on your MacBook. These small adjustments make a significant difference, enhancing usability and ensuring that your MacBook adapts to your specific needs.

Chapter 8: Troubleshooting Common Issues

8.1 Resolving Wi-Fi and Connectivity Issues

Encountering Wi-Fi or connectivity problems on your MacBook can be frustrating, but there are several straightforward steps you can take to troubleshoot these issues. Start by checking your Wi-Fi connection in the menu bar at the top of the screen. If the Wi-Fi icon shows a weak signal or appears disconnected, try toggling Wi-Fi off and on by clicking the icon. Often, a quick reset of the Wi-Fi connection can resolve minor connectivity problems.

If toggling Wi-Fi doesn't work, verify that your MacBook is connected to the correct network. Click the Wi-Fi icon in the menu bar to view available networks and ensure you're connected to your preferred one. If prompted, enter the correct password. Sometimes, being too far from the router can cause weak signals; if possible, move closer to the Wi-Fi source to see if that improves connectivity.

Restarting both your MacBook and the Wi-Fi router is another effective step, as it refreshes network connections. Turn off your router, wait for about 30 seconds, then power it back on. Once the router is fully operational, restart your MacBook and check if the Wi-Fi issue has been resolved. If the problem persists, use macOS's built-in diagnostic tool by holding down the "Option" key and clicking the Wi-Fi icon, then selecting "Open Wireless Diagnostics." Follow the prompts to diagnose potential network issues, as this tool can identify and recommend solutions for common connectivity problems.

8.2 Troubleshooting Software Updates

Software updates are essential for keeping your MacBook secure and running smoothly, but they can sometimes encounter issues. If you're unable to download or install an update, start by checking your internet connection. A stable connection is necessary for downloading updates, so ensure you're connected to Wi-Fi or a reliable network source. Once connected, go to "System Preferences" and select "Software Update" to check for any available updates.

If the update appears but won't download or install, try restarting your MacBook. This often clears temporary issues that may be interfering with the update process. After restarting, go back to Software Update and attempt the installation again. If you're still having trouble, make sure your MacBook has enough storage space for the update.

You can check available storage by clicking the Apple menu, choosing "About This Mac," and selecting the "Storage" tab. If storage is low, consider deleting unnecessary files or moving items to an external drive to create space.

For updates that partially download but won't complete, you may need to reset the Software Update cache. Open Finder, go to "Go" in the menu bar, select "Go to Folder," and enter `~/Library/Updates`. Deleting the files in this folder can clear any incomplete downloads, allowing you to start fresh. Return to "System Preferences" and retry the update process. If issues persist, Apple's website or support team can provide further assistance with difficult updates.

8.3 Fixing Application Crashes

If an application on your MacBook crashes frequently or refuses to open, there are several steps you can take to resolve this. Start by closing the app completely.

Go to the Apple menu, choose "Force Quit," select the problematic app, and click "Force Quit." After forcing the app to close, reopen it to see if the problem has been resolved.

Sometimes, app crashes are due to corrupted preferences or settings files. To address this, open Finder, click on "Go" in the menu bar, and select "Go to Folder." Enter `~/Library/Preferences`, then search for the preferences file associated with the app (it typically has the app's name followed by ".plist"). Deleting this file can reset the app's preferences, which may resolve crashing issues. After deleting the file, reopen the app to see if it works properly.

If the app continues to crash, it's possible that an outdated or incompatible version is the cause. Open the App Store, go to the "Updates" tab, and check if there's an update available for the app.

Updating to the latest version can fix bugs or compatibility issues that may be causing the crashes. If the app is not from the App Store, check the developer's website for any updates or patches.

In some cases, uninstalling and reinstalling the app can fix persistent crashes. To uninstall, go to Finder, open the "Applications" folder, find the app, and drag it to the Trash. Empty the Trash to remove it completely, then reinstall the app from the App Store or the developer's website. A fresh installation can often resolve underlying issues that cause crashes.

8.4 Managing Battery Health and Charging Tips

To keep your MacBook's battery in good health, there are several best practices you can follow. Monitoring battery health is essential for ensuring longevity, and macOS provides an easy way to do this.

Click the battery icon in the menu bar, then select "Battery Preferences." Here, you'll see an option to view "Battery Health," which shows the overall condition of your battery. If it's listed as "Normal," your battery is in good shape, but if you see "Service Recommended," it may be time to consult Apple Support or a technician.

To maintain battery health, avoid letting the battery drain completely. It's best to keep the battery level between 20% and 80% when possible, as this range minimizes wear on the battery cells. When charging, avoid leaving your MacBook plugged in for extended periods, as this can cause the battery to remain at 100%, which may decrease its lifespan over time. The macOS "Optimized Battery Charging" feature, found in Battery Preferences, helps prevent overcharging by learning your charging habits and reducing full charging until you need it.

Using low-power mode can also conserve battery life, especially if you're working away from a power source. In Battery Preferences, enable "Low Power Mode" to reduce background processes and lower screen brightness, which can extend battery life during long work sessions. Additionally, reducing the screen brightness manually and closing unnecessary apps or browser tabs can help conserve battery life.

If you're experiencing rapid battery drain, check for apps that consume a lot of power. Click on the battery icon in the menu bar, where macOS will list "Apps Using Significant Energy." Closing these apps or switching to less resource-intensive alternatives can improve battery performance. Running periodic software updates also helps, as updates often include battery optimization improvements.

By following these charging and usage tips, you can help maintain your MacBook's battery health, ensuring it remains reliable and long-lasting. Taking these steps regularly can lead to improved battery performance, making your MacBook more dependable for daily tasks.

Chapter 9: Exploring Advanced MacBook Features (Optional)

9.1 Using iCloud for Backup and Synchronization

iCloud provides a secure and convenient way to back up and synchronize your MacBook data across all your Apple devices. When you enable iCloud on your MacBook, your files, photos, contacts, and calendar events are saved to Apple's cloud servers, making them accessible on any device signed in with your Apple ID. To set up iCloud, open "System Preferences" and select "Apple ID." From there, navigate to "iCloud" and choose the items you'd like to sync, such as photos, documents, or Safari bookmarks.

Enabling these options ensures that your data is stored safely in the cloud and synchronized across all your Apple devices.

iCloud Drive is especially useful for keeping documents and files accessible. By moving files to the iCloud Drive folder on your MacBook, they become available on any other device linked to the same Apple ID, including your iPhone or iPad. This is ideal for those who switch between devices often, as it eliminates the need to manually transfer files. Additionally, the "Optimize Mac Storage" option within iCloud settings allows you to save space by storing full versions of files in the cloud, while keeping smaller versions on your MacBook until you need them.

Backing up photos with iCloud Photos is another helpful feature, particularly if you have a large photo library. By enabling iCloud Photos, every photo you take or import is automatically uploaded to iCloud and accessible on all devices.

iCloud Photos also keeps your edits synchronized, so any changes made to a photo on one device are reflected everywhere. This feature provides peace of mind, knowing your photos are safely backed up and easy to access at any time.

9.2 Setting Up Automations with Siri Shortcuts

Siri Shortcuts bring a new level of efficiency to your MacBook by allowing you to automate tasks with simple voice commands or shortcuts. To create shortcuts, open the Shortcuts app, which comes pre-installed on your MacBook. Here, you can create personalized automations by combining actions from different apps into a single shortcut.

For example, you could set up a "Good Morning" shortcut that reads out your calendar events, checks the weather, and opens Safari to your preferred news site with one command.

Shortcuts offer a wide variety of actions, so you can tailor them to suit your daily routines or specific workflows.

To create a shortcut, click the "+" button in the Shortcuts app and choose from available actions, such as sending a message, adjusting settings, or playing music. You can link multiple actions together, setting up complex shortcuts to handle multi-step processes effortlessly. Once saved, these shortcuts can be triggered through Siri, by clicking the shortcut in the Shortcuts app, or even by setting up automations based on time or location.

Siri Shortcuts is also a powerful tool for professionals, as it enables you to streamline repetitive tasks. If you frequently email clients or team members, you can create a shortcut that drafts a new email, fills in the subject line, and attaches a relevant file. With just one click or voice command, the shortcut handles these actions automatically, saving you time and effort.

By exploring the available options within the Shortcuts app, you can create personalized automations that make your MacBook work more efficiently.

9.3 Utilizing Split Screen and Mission Control

Split Screen and Mission Control are features that help improve multitasking and organization on your MacBook. Split Screen allows you to work in two applications side by side, making it easier to reference information in one app while working in another. To enter Split Screen mode, open an app and click and hold the green button in the top-left corner of the window. You'll then see one side of the screen darken, prompting you to drag the window to either side. Once positioned, select another open application to fill the other half of the screen, creating a split view.

Using Split Screen is beneficial for tasks that require comparing data, like writing a report while referencing a web page or editing photos while viewing an inspiration image. You can adjust the size of each window by dragging the vertical line dividing the two apps, allowing you to customize the layout for your needs. To exit Split Screen mode, move your cursor to the top of the screen and click the green button on either window.

Mission Control, on the other hand, provides an overview of all open windows, desktops, and full-screen apps, helping you stay organized when you have multiple applications running. To access Mission Control, swipe up with three or four fingers on the trackpad, or press the F3 key. Mission Control shows all your active windows at once, arranged in a layout that makes it easy to switch between them or create separate workspaces.

In addition to viewing open windows, Mission Control allows you to set up multiple desktops, known as "Spaces."

For example, you might dedicate one Space to work-related apps and another to personal browsing, reducing distractions. You can drag windows between Spaces or create full-screen views for apps you want to keep separate. These features make multitasking more manageable, helping you organize your work and switch contexts seamlessly.

9.4 Exploring macOS Updates and New Features

Apple regularly releases updates for macOS, each bringing new features, improvements, and security enhancements to your MacBook. Staying up to date ensures that your MacBook benefits from the latest advancements, including performance optimizations and added functionalities. To check for updates, open "System Preferences" and select "Software Update." If a new version of macOS is available, you'll see an option to download and install it.

Regularly updating your system also protects against security vulnerabilities, as Apple frequently patches any known issues with each release.

Each macOS update often includes new features designed to enhance productivity and usability. For example, recent updates have introduced improvements like a refined Notification Center, customizable widgets, and better integration with iOS devices. Widgets allow you to add mini-apps to your desktop, showing information at a glance, such as calendar events, weather, or reminders. Customizing your widgets can make accessing key information quicker and more convenient, without needing to open full applications.

Updates may also bring improvements to the Messages and Safari apps. Recent macOS versions have expanded the Messages app with features like pinned conversations, reactions, and improved group messaging, making it easier to communicate with friends, family, and colleagues. Safari often receives performance upgrades and privacy enhancements, ensuring faster browsing and better protection from online tracking. Apple also tends to introduce new privacy settings with each macOS version, giving users greater control over data-sharing permissions.

Staying informed about macOS updates not only keeps your MacBook secure but also helps you make the most of Apple's evolving ecosystem. Each update is designed to refine the user experience and make daily tasks more efficient, so exploring new features and settings after each update can reveal tools that improve your workflow. With each release, macOS aims to enhance your MacBook's functionality, making it a valuable companion for work, creativity, and personal use.

Chapter 10: Security and Privacy Best Practices

10.1 Understanding macOS Security Updates

macOS security updates play a crucial role in protecting your MacBook from emerging threats and vulnerabilities. Apple regularly releases these updates to address security weaknesses, enhance system stability, and improve overall performance. Staying up-to-date with the latest security patches is essential, as each update contains fixes for potential risks that may not be immediately visible but could impact your data and privacy. To check for available updates, open "System Preferences" and select "Software Update."

When an update is available, click "Update Now" to install it, and consider enabling automatic updates to keep your MacBook secure without requiring manual checks.

Apple's approach to security also includes frequent updates to the Safari browser, which help protect against online threats, such as phishing websites and malicious ads. Regularly updating your browser ensures you have the latest security features to guard against these types of attacks. Additionally, macOS updates often include improved encryption for data protection and enhanced security protocols to keep your information safe while browsing, emailing, and managing files.

By keeping macOS current, you reduce the risk of unauthorized access and maintain a secure environment for personal and work data.

10.2 Enabling and Managing Privacy Settings

macOS provides robust privacy settings to help you control what information apps and websites can access, protecting your personal data.

To review and adjust privacy settings, open "System Preferences" and select "Security & Privacy." Under the "Privacy" tab, you'll find options to manage permissions for various types of data, including location, contacts, photos, and microphone access. For each category, you can see which apps have requested access and enable or disable permissions as needed.

Location Services, found within Privacy settings, allow you to control which apps can use your location. If there's no need for an app to track your whereabouts, you can disable its access to enhance privacy. For example, you might allow location access for mapping applications but restrict it for social media apps. Another important feature is the ability to manage permissions for your camera and microphone, ensuring that only trusted apps can access these components.

This level of control prevents unauthorized access and gives you peace of mind when using apps that rely on audio or video.

Safari also includes privacy features that help protect against online tracking. By going to Safari's "Preferences" and selecting the "Privacy" tab, you can enable settings like "Prevent Cross-Site Tracking" and "Block All Cookies" to limit how websites track your activity. These settings reduce targeted ads and limit data-sharing across sites, preserving your privacy while browsing. macOS also provides options for managing app permissions in general, giving you full control over which applications can access data stored on your MacBook.

10.3 Backing Up Data with Time Machine

Backing up your MacBook regularly is essential for safeguarding important files, photos, and documents against data loss.

Time Machine, a built-in macOS feature, makes it easy to create automatic backups to an external drive, ensuring you have a recent copy of your data should anything happen to your device.

To set up Time Machine, connect an external hard drive to your MacBook, then open "System Preferences" and select "Time Machine." Choose "Select Backup Disk," then select your external drive and click "Use Disk." Time Machine will begin creating hourly backups, storing daily snapshots, and preserving older versions of files as long as space allows.

Time Machine's incremental backup system is beneficial because it allows you to retrieve specific versions of files from different dates. For instance, if you accidentally delete a file or need to recover an earlier version, you can open Time Machine, navigate to the date in question, and restore the file with just a few clicks.

This feature is especially helpful for recovering documents you may have accidentally modified or deleted.

Time Machine backups can also be invaluable when transitioning to a new MacBook. By restoring from a backup, you can transfer all your data, apps, and settings, making the new device feel like your old one. Additionally, Time Machine's backups are encrypted if you choose to enable this option during setup, adding an extra layer of security to protect your data on the external drive. Regularly backing up with Time Machine ensures that you have a reliable copy of your files, minimizing the risk of data loss in the event of hardware failure or accidental deletion.

10.4 Protecting Against Phishing and Malware

Phishing and malware are common threats in today's digital world, and macOS includes several features to help protect against these risks. Phishing involves deceptive emails or messages that trick users into revealing personal information, while malware refers to malicious software that can harm your device or steal data.

To safeguard against these threats, start by being cautious about unsolicited emails or messages that ask for sensitive information. Legitimate companies will never request personal data like passwords or credit card details via email. If you receive a suspicious email, avoid clicking links or downloading attachments, as they may contain malware.

To further protect against phishing, macOS Safari has a "Fraudulent Website Warning" setting, which alerts you if you attempt to access a potentially dangerous site. This feature, found under Safari's "Preferences" in the "Security" tab, checks URLs against a list of known phishing sites and warns you before loading suspicious content.

Keeping Safari and macOS updated also ensures that your system benefits from the latest protections against phishing attacks and malware.

In addition to phishing defenses, macOS includes built-in malware protection called XProtect. This feature automatically checks for known malware each time an application is opened, blocking malicious software from running on your MacBook. XProtect updates regularly in the background, ensuring your system remains protected from the latest threats without requiring any action on your part. Furthermore, macOS Gatekeeper is another security layer that restricts the installation of unverified apps from unknown sources.

Gatekeeper helps prevent malware by allowing only apps downloaded from the App Store or identified developers to run on your device, reducing the risk of installing harmful software.

If you'd like additional protection, you can also consider installing reputable antivirus software.

Many antivirus programs offer extra features, such as web protection and real-time scanning, which can provide an extra level of security for online activities and downloads. By combining macOS's built-in defenses with safe browsing habits and optional antivirus software, you can create a robust line of defense against phishing and malware, helping keep your MacBook secure and your data protected.

Conclusion

As you reach the end of this guide, take a moment to recognize just how far you've come in mastering your MacBook. From the initial setup to navigating advanced features, you've explored the essential aspects of using this device effectively and confidently. Whether you're new to the MacBook or just looking to deepen your understanding, these chapters have equipped you with practical skills to make your MacBook an invaluable tool in your daily life.

Reflecting on what you've learned, you can now handle the basics with ease, from organizing files in Finder to managing tasks with Reminders, using Calendar for appointments, and staying connected through email and FaceTime.

You've also gained insights into more advanced tools, such as iCloud synchronization and Siri Shortcuts, that streamline your workflows and make the MacBook experience truly personalized. By following the security and privacy tips shared in this guide, you can explore the internet with greater confidence, knowing your data and device are protected.

As for next steps, feel free to revisit any chapter or section that you found particularly helpful or that you'd like to explore in more detail. The flexibility of the MacBook means there's always something new to discover, and Apple frequently releases updates and enhancements to macOS. Keeping an eye out for these updates allows you to continue learning and take advantage of new features that can improve your experience.

To expand your skills, consider exploring additional resources tailored to your interests.

Apple's official website and support pages offer a wealth of information on various features, as well as troubleshooting tips and instructional videos. Apple's "Today at Apple" sessions, available online or in Apple Stores, provide hands-on learning experiences led by Apple experts, where you can get personalized advice and tips on making the most of your MacBook.

In addition, online communities like the Apple Support Community and other tech forums are excellent places to find solutions, ask questions, and learn from other users' experiences. Websites, video tutorials, and user groups dedicated to MacBooks offer a supportive environment where you can share knowledge and gain inspiration for creative and practical ways to use your device.

With this guide and these resources, you're now well-prepared to continue learning, exploring, and confidently using your MacBook.

Embrace this journey, knowing that your MacBook is designed to be a flexible tool that grows with you. As you continue to build your skills, your MacBook will become not only a device but also a reliable companion, enhancing your productivity, keeping you connected, and supporting you in whatever you choose to pursue.

www.ingramcontent.com/pod-product-compliance
Lightning Source LLC
LaVergne TN
LVHW051710050326
832903LV00032B/4123